PowerPhonics™

Boats That Float

Learning the OA Sound

Abigail Richter

The Rosen Publishing Group's
PowerKids Press™
New York

Boats float on water.

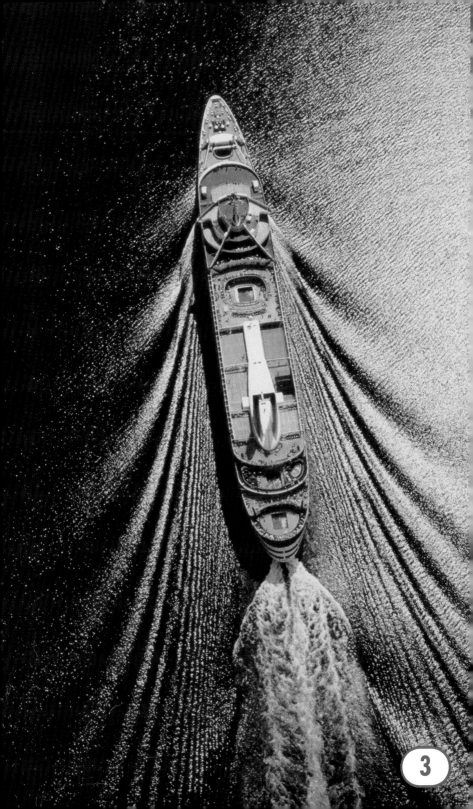

Little boats float.

Big boats float.

Boats can float on a river.

9

Boats can float on a lake.

Boats can float on the sea.

Boats cannot float on roads.

Boats can carry loads.

Boats can carry other boats.

Boats can carry people.

Word List

boats
float
loads
roads

Instructional Guide

Note to Instructors:
One of the essential skills that enable a young child to read is the ability to associate letter-sound symbols and blend these sounds to form words. Phonics instruction can teach children a system that will help them decode unfamiliar words and, in turn, enhance their word-recognition skills. We offer a phonics-based series of books that are easy to read and understand. Each book pairs words and pictures that reinforce specific phonetic sounds in a logical sequence. Topics are based on curriculum goals appropriate for early readers in the areas of science, social studies, and health.

Letter/Sound: oa — Have the child name words with the **long o** sound. List the words in columns according to their spelling (**oa** as in *boat,* **ow** as in *low,* **o-e** as in **hope**). Have the child underline **oa, ow,** or **o** in each word. Ask them to circle the silent letter in each word.

Phonics Activities: Ask the child to name a **long o** word to complete the following oral sentences: *When it's cold, I wear a (coat). An animal that's good at climbing is a mountain (goat). I wash my hands with (soap). Horses eat hay and (oats). I like jelly on my (toast).* List the child's responses. Have them underline **oa** in each word.
- Pronounce the following compound words as you write them on a chalkboard or dry-erase board. Ask the child to tell whether they see and hear **long o** near the beginning or the end of the word: *riverboat, oatmeal, tugboat, boathouse, houseboat, sailboat, lifeboat.* As the child responds, list the words in two columns according to where the **long o** sound occurs. Have the child underline **oa** in each of them.
- Pronounce the following words, having the child name the consonant sounds they hear at the beginning and at the end of them: *coal, float, roar, soap, coat, goat.* List the words and have the child underline **oa** in each of them.

Additional Resources:
- Saunders-Smith, Gail. *Boats.* Danbury, CT: Children's Press, 1998.
- Sullivan Hill, Lee. *On Water.* Minneapolis, MN: The Lerner Publishing Group, 1999.
- Walker, Pamela. *Boat Rides.* Danbury, CT: Children's Press, 2000.

Published in 2002 by The Rosen Publishing Group, Inc.
29 East 21st Street, New York, NY 10010

Book Design: Ron A. Churley

Photo Credits: Cover © Chad Ehlers/International Stock; p. 3 © Telegraph Colour Library/FPG International; p. 5 © John Terence Turner/FPG International; p. 7 © Bill Bachmann/Index Stock; pp. 9, 11, 13, 19 © SuperStock; p. 15 © Allen Russell/Index Stock; p. 17 © Steve Dunwell/Image Bank; p. 21 © Jeff Schultz/Index Stock.

Library of Congress Cataloging-in-Publication Data

Richter, Abigail, 1971-
    Boats that float : learning the OA sound / Abigail Richter.
        p. cm. — (Power phonics/phonics for the real world)
    ISBN 0-8239-5935-X (library binding)
    ISBN 0-8239-8280-7 (paperback)
    6 pack ISBN 0-8239-9248-9
    1. Boats and boating—Juvenile literature. [1. Boats and boating.
    2. Ships.] I. Title. II. Series.
    VM150 .R487 2001
    428.1—dc21
                                                2001000660

Manufactured in the United States of America